ARTIST TRANSCRIPTIONS

TRANSCRIBED BY GREG FISHMAN

CW00538617

STAN G

B♭ TENOR SAXOPHONE

CONTENTS

Cover photo: Ray Avery

HAL•LEONARD® CORPORATION

7777 W. BLUEMOUND RD. P.O. BOX 13819 MILWAUKEE, WI 53213

ABOUT THE AUTHOR

Tenor saxophonist, Greg Fishman, was born in 1967, and is a graduate of DePaul University, Chicago, Illinois. He studied with Joe Henderson, David Liebman, Hal Galper, Mark Colby, Joe Daley, Alan Swain, and Larry Combs. He has performed with Louis Bellson, Clark Terry, Don Menza, Ira Sullivan, Bobby Shew, Eddie Higgins, Larry Novak, and Rusty Jones. He was the winner of the 1992 North American Saxophone Alliance's Young Artists Competition. Currently freelancing with his own quartet in Chicago area jazz clubs, he also finds time to record with such artists as Kirsten Gustafson, whose current CD is entitled *You Taught My Heart To Sing*. Mr. Fishman teaches jazz improvisation privately, and also through several school systems in the Chicago area.

DEDICATION

Since discovering the beauty of Stan Getz's music in 1985, I was so inspired, that I spent the past eight years studying, absorbing, and learning from it. Throughout our personal meetings and phone conversations, his encouragement of my transcriptions was both an honor and a privilege.

This book is dedicated to the memory of Stan Getz.

ABOUT THE BOOK

There were several cases in which the melody was sung on the recording from which these solos were taken. "Quiet Nights" and "It Might As Well Be Spring" were sung by Astrud Gilberto. For each of these I have transcribed the melodies and adapted them for tenor saxophone.

"Desafinado" and "The Girl From Ipanema" were also sung on the record. However, Getz's solos on both of these tunes were basically 80% melody with the addition of some very eloquent variation on Getz's part. I felt that to print the original melody and then Getz's solo would be redundant.

The only other case in which the melody was not included is for "All The Things You Are." This particular solo was taken from a *Jazz At The Philharmonic* recording in which Don Byas, Coleman Hawkins, Getz, and Dizzy Gillespie are all playing bits and pieces of the melody at one time.

BIOGRAPHY

Stan Getz was born in Philadelphia on February 2, 1927 and grew up in New York. At age 15 he received his first professional job with Jack Teagarden's band. He stayed with Teagarden for nine months and settled in Los Angeles when the band disbanded in 1943. He performed with Stan Kenton in 1944-45, Benny Goodman in 1945-46, and in 1947 he joined Woody Herman's band. In late December of 1948 he recorded his famous "Early Autumn" solo which launched his career practically overnight. He left Woody Herman in early 1949 and returned to New York to lead his own quartet.

Throughout the 1950s, Getz led groups introducing such personnel as Horace Silver, Al Haig, Tommy Potter, Jimmy Raney, Roy Haynes, Duke Jordan, Bob Brookmeyer, and Lou Levy. Even though the material he played consisted mostly of standards, some bebop tunes were also played. Getz was nicknamed "The Sound," and was widely known for his beautiful ballads. His solos during the early 1950s had an extremely introspective quality. "Yesterdays," from the album *The Complete Roost Sessions, Vol. 1* (Vogue VG 651), is a good example.

While critics labeled Getz "Cool," he was beyond categorization. Listen to the ferocity with which he plays "Parker 51" or "Move" from the *Storyville* sessions of 1952. (Mosaic MD3-131). Toward the end of the '50s, Getz's tone became much deeper, and the character of his playing acquired an earthy quality. "Blues For Mary Jane" from the album *The Steamer* (Verve MG-V 8294), depicts this quality.

Getz moved to Denmark in 1958 and recorded some excellent records (available on the Rarities label, from England) with bassist Oscar Pettiford. During Getz's absence from the American Jazz scene, however, Sonny Rollins and John Coltrane became the most popular tenor players.

Getz marked his return to the United States with a breathtaking album called *Focus* (Verve 821 982-2). The music, for strings and rhythm section, was written by Eddie Sauter; however, Getz's part was completely improvised. This was Getz's favorite record. Although *Focus* was a complete artistic success, it did not bring back the popularity he had enjoyed throughout the 1950s.

Upon the release of *Jazz Samba* (Verve V6-8432) in April of 1962, Getz's popularity once again soared. *Jazz Samba* entered the pop charts on September 15, 1962, reached the number one position, and stayed on the charts for 70 weeks! This album earned Getz a Grammy award for Best Jazz Performance. In 1964, *Getz/Gilberto* (Verve V6-8545) reached number two on the pop chart, won eight Grammy Awards, and gave the world "The Girl From Ipanema." The early to middle '60s were considered to be the Bossa Nova years. Getz was a natural for this sensuous, melodic, bittersweet music from Brazil, and his playing was marked by extremely inventive and subtle use of articulation and tonal shadings.

The commercial success of the Bossa Nova never dulled Getz's sense of creativity. In 1964, at the height of the Bossa Nova fad, Getz recorded a straight ahead jazz album with Bill Evans and Elvin Jones. (Verve 833 802-2). Getz' working group during this time period performed both straight ahead jazz and bossa novas. This group, which included vibist Gary Burton, can be heard on the album *Getz Au Go Go*, (Verve 821 725-2).

By the middle 1960s, Getz formed yet another new group consisting of Chick Corea, Steve Swallow, and Roy Haynes. The album, *Sweet Rain* (Verve 815-054-2), is an excellent example of this group's musical interpretation. Interestingly, the night before the session, both Haynes and Swallow came down with the flu. On the morning of the recording session Getz hired Ron Carter and Grady Tate to play on the record. This record is regarded as one of Getz's best albums. Other groups during the late '60s included Jack DeJohnette, Richard Beirach, and Miroslav Vitous.

By the early 1970s, Getz's playing became more aggressive. By 1975 Getz's group consisted of Albert Dailey, Clint Houston, and Billy Hart. This explosive quartet can be heard, with Getz at the top of his form, on an album aptly titled, *The Master.* (Columbia FC-38272). In 1976, pianist Joanne Brackeen became part of Getz's working group. The group can be heard on *Live at Montmartre, Vols. 1 & 2* (Steeplechase 8CCD-31073 & 31074).

Another World, (Columbia BL-35514) recorded in 1977, marked a new direction for Getz. This group included Andy Laverne, Mike Richmond, Billy Hart, and Efrain Toro. Differing from Getz's previous efforts, this was an electric group: electric bass, synthesizers, and even the occasional use of an Echoplex by Getz himself.

The 1980s was a decade of renaissance for Getz. He returned to an all acoustic quartet playing many of the standard tunes he had recorded in the 1950s. It's fascinating to hear how Getz's style changed when you compare standards, such as the 1952 and 1981 versions of "Body & Soul." The album *Pure Getz* (Concord CCD 4188) is a masterpiece. It features Jim McNeely, Marc Johnson, Victor Lewis, and Billy Hart. Selections include Bill Evan's beautiful waltz, "Very Early," as well as the Bud Powell classic, "Tempus Fugit," both of which are included in this book.

Starting in 1986, Kenny Barron became Getz's new pianist. Getz's working band in the 1980s consisted of Kenny Barron, George Mraz or Rufus Reid, and Victor Lewis. The albums *Voyage* (Blackhawk BKH 511-2), *Anniversary* (EmArcy 838 769-2), and *Serenity* (EmArcy 838 770-2), are an excellent representation of this quartet.

In 1990, Getz collaborated with Herb Alpert and Eddie del Barrio in producing *Apasionado*. The album is similar to *Focus* in that Getz's part, for the majority of the album was total improvisation supported by a large ensemble background. Getz shows again his uncanny ability to sound at home in any setting without sacrificing any of his own artistic qualities.

The last record that Getz recorded, *People Time*, (Verve 314 510 823-2) is a duet with Kenny Barron. It was recorded just three months before Getz's death due to cancer on June 6, 1991. While listening to the album, one can hear the pain, courage, love, and beauty that Stan Getz possessed.

An uncompromising artist, never content to rest on his laurels, Stan Getz was always searching and expanding his music. The following quote best describes Getz's musical genius: "My life is music - and in some vague, mysterious and subconscious way I have always been driven by a taut inner spring which has propelled me to almost compulsively reach for perfection in music, often, in fact, mostly at the expense of everything else in my life."

STYLE ANALYSIS

I use the term "Melodic Structuralist" to describe the melodic aspect of Getz's playing. Although Getz's style underwent many changes throughout his career, the aspect that remained constant throughout was an unwavering use of melodic ideas and development of those ideas within each solo.

The "Melodic" part of the term describes the lyrical quality of Getz's improvisations. In essence, his improvisations could be interpreted as melodies themselves.

The "Structuralist" part of the term may at first seem strange, especially when referring to Getz. After all, he was such a natural sounding player. When listening to his solos, one doesn't hear Getz playing many "licks." Getz was quoted as saying, "I've never played a note I didn't mean." While one could isolate a phrase from any of the solos in this book and practice it out of context, one should understand that Getz didn't conceive the idea as a lick. He conceived it as one small part in the development of an entire solo.

Theme and variation were key elements of Getz's style. In addition to the usual introduction of a short theme immediately followed with development, Getz had a unique way of creating variations on the same theme throughout the entire solo. For example, in "Split Kick" compare the 10th and 26th measures of the form. In each solo chorus see how inventively Getz kept the essence of the original melody while creating his own melodic variations on the original.

Getz used many common, everyday intervallic structures such as major 7th, minor 7th, half-diminished, diminished, and augmented chords. In his soloing, his use of these structures is what makes them unique. By placing these structures in a great variety of settings, their context is changed. Over a B♭ major chord, Getz would play an A major triad; or he may have played a Cmin7 chord against a C7♯9, B♭min7, Amin7♭5, A♭Maj7, Gmin7, G♭13♭9♯11, Fmin7, E♭Maj7, Dmin7♭5, or D♭Maj7♯11.

A master at foreshadowing chord changes, Getz would frequently outline these chord changes one to two measures early. This proved to be a great help in leading the rhythm section to play the changes and alterations he was hearing. If it appears as though some of the notes Getz played do not correspond with the chord immediately above the measure, look ahead one to two measures. For example, if a phrase ends with an A♭, and the chord above it is a C7, it may very well be a ♯5 (G♯) of the C7 chord. However, if the next measure is "Fmin," you should also consider that he was probably foreshadowing the F minor chord before it actually arrived.

Extremely resourceful with his phrases, Getz always created different ways to play the same basic theme. The technique he used to achieve this variety was to displace the entire phrase by one to four beats. Stan was comfortable playing a phrase on any of eight starting places; the downbeats of one, two, three, and four, and the upbeats as well. It was this ability to place a phrase at any of these eight starting points that helped make Getz's solos sound so fresh and spontaneous.

Other aspects of Getz's playing, such as time feel, tone, articulation, and dynamics, are difficult to describe in words. I suggest very careful listening to the recordings to get an understanding of Getz's concept for each of these topics. Try listening for each of these aspects separately on a recording. Then listen to how Getz makes them all work together congruently.

SPECIAL NOTATION

At times in this book, 4th line "D" is marked with the letter "S" above it. This is an indication to use the side "D" fingering (palm key) without the octave key depressed.

EARLY AUTUMN

Words by JOHNNY MERCE
Music by RALPH BURN
and WOODY HERMA

Bb TENOR SAXOPHONE

OUT OF NOWHERE

Words by EDWARD HEYMAN
Music by JOHNNY GREEN

Bb TENOR SAXOPHONE

STRIKE UP THE BAND

Words by IRA GERSHWIN
Music by GEORGE GERSHWIN

B♭ TENOR SAXOPHONE

SPLIT KICK

Bb TENOR SAXOPHONE

By HORACE SILVER

18

* S = SIDE KEY

BODY AND SOUL ✓
(1952 Version)

Words by EDWARD HEYMAN,
ROBERT SOUR and FRANK EYTON
Music by JOHN GREEN

Bb TENOR SAXOPHONE

I'M GLAD THERE IS YOU
(In This World Of Ordinary People)

Words and Music by
PAUL MADEIRA and JIMMY DORSEY

♭ TENOR SAXOPHONE

= SIDE KEY

ALL THE THINGS YOU ARE

(From "VERY WARM FOR MAY")

Bb TENOR SAXOPHONE

Lyrics by OSCAR HAMMERSTEIN II
Music by JEROME KERN

THE GIRL FROM IPANEMA
(Garôta De Ipanema)

Bb TENOR SAXOPHONE

Original Words by VINICIUS DE MORAES
English Words by NORMAN GIMBEL
Music by ANTONIO CARLOS JOBIM

✱ S = SIDE KEY

MCA music publishing

DESAFINADO
(Slightly Out Of Tune)

English Words by JON HENDRICKS
and JESSIE CAVANAUGH
Original Words by NEWTON MENDONCA
Music by ANTONIO CARLOS JOBIM

Bb TENOR SAXOPHONE

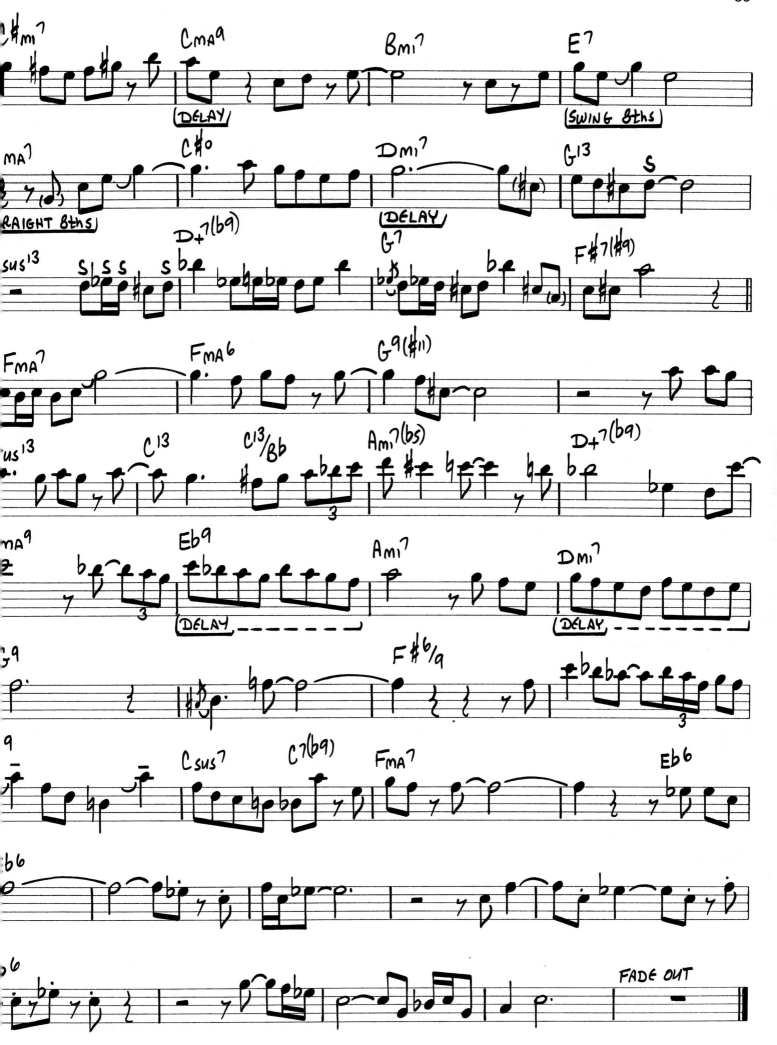

IT MIGHT AS WELL BE SPRING

(From "STATE FAIR")

Bb TENOR SAXOPHONE

Lyrics by OSCAR HAMMERSTEIN
Music by RICHARD RODGERS

NIGHT AND DAY

Words and Music by COLE PORTER

Bb TENOR SAXOPHONE

* S = SIDE KEY

QUIET NIGHTS OF QUIET STARS
(Corcovado)

English Words by GENE LE
Original Words and Music
ANTONIO CARLOS JOE

Bb TENOR SAXOPHONE

MCA music publishing

INVITATION

Bb TENOR SAXOPHONE

Words by PAUL FRANCIS WEBSTER
Music by BRONISLAU KAPER

48

50

LOVER MAN
(Oh, Where Can You Be?)

By JIMMY DAVIS, ROGER "RAM" RAMIREZ
and JIMMY SHERMAN

♭ TENOR SAXOPHONE

MCA music publishing

56

BODY AND SOUL

(1981 Version)

Words by EDWARD HEYMAN
ROBERT SOUR and FRANK EYTON
Music by JOHN GREEN

B♭ TENOR SAXOPHONE

ON THE UP AND UP

By JIM McNEELY

Bb TENOR SAXOPHONE

FR = FRONT "F" KEY

TEMPUS FUGIT

By EARL BUD POWELL

TENOR SAXOPHONE

VERY EARLY

Lyric by CAROL HALL
Music by BILL EVANS

B♭ TENOR SAXOPHONE

YESTERDAYS

Words by OTTO HARBACH
Music by JEROME KERN

♭ TENOR SAXOPHONE

COBA

By STAN GETZ, HERB ALPERT
and EDDIE DEL BARRIO

TENOR SAXOPHONE

S = SIDE KEY

82

88

DISCOGRAPHY

TITLE	YEAR	TITLE
Early Autumn	1948	Capitol Jazz Classics Vol. 9 - M-11034
Out Of Nowhere	1950	Complete Roost Sessions Vol. 1 CD: Vogue VG651 600128 LP: Roost 596, Jam 5007, Vogue VJD 573
Strike Up The Band	1950	Complete Roost Sessions Vol. 1 CD: Vogue VG651 600128 LP: Vogue VJD 573, Roost RLP-402
Split Kick	1951	Complete Roost Sessions Vol. 1 CD: Vogue VG651 600128 LP: Vogue VJD 573, Roost 526 & RLP-417
Body And Soul (Version 1)	1952	Stan Getz Plays CD: Verve 833 535-2 LP: Verve MGV-8133
I'm Glad There Is You	1957	Stan Getz & The Oscar Peterson Trio CD: Verve 827 826-2 LP: Verve MGV-8251
All The Things You Are	1960	JATP In Europe LP: Verve V-8539
Girl From Ipanema, The	1963	CD: The Bossa Nova Years - Verve 823 611-2 LP: Getz/Gilberto - Verve V6-8545
Desafinado (Slightly Out Of Tune)	1964	CD: The Bossa Nova Years - Verve 823 611-2 LP: Getz/Gilberto - Verve V6-8545
It Might As Well Be Spring	1964	CD: The Bossa Nova Years - Verve 823 611-2 CD: Getz Au Go Go - Verve 821 725-2 LP: Getz Au Go Go - Verve V6-8600
Night And Day	1964	Stan Getz & Bill Evans CD: Verve 833 802-2 LP: Verve V6-8833
Quiet Nights Of Quiet Stars (Corcovado)	1964	CD: The Bossa Nova Years - Verve 823 611-2 CD: Getz Au Go Go - Verve 821 725-2 LP: Getz Au Go Go - Verve V6-8600
Invitation	1975	The Master CD: CBS 467138 2 LP: Columbia FC38272
Lover Man	1975	The Master CD: CBS 467138 2 LP: Columbia FC38272
Body And Soul (Version 2)	1981	Billy Highstreet Samba CD: Emarcy 838 771-2
On The Up And Up	1982	Pure Getz CD: Concord CCD 4188 LP: CJ-188
Tempus Fugit	1982	Pure Getz CD: Concord CCD 4188 LP: CJ-188
Very Early	1982	Pure Getz CD: Concord CCD 4188 LP: CJ-188
Yesterdays	1986	CD: Voyage - Blackhawk BKH 511-2
Coba	1990	CD: Apasionado - A & M 75021 5297 2